GadChick Presents:

My First MacBook / MacBook Air

*A Beginners Guide to Unplugging You
Windows PC and Becoming a Mac User*

Andie Campbell

GadChick Books

www.gadchick.com

Cover Image © stockphotographer - Fotolia.com

D1421683

Table of Contents

About GadChick

Thank you for buying (or sampling) this book. If you have never heard of us before, hello—it's nice to meet you!

GadChick is a magazine and blog written by women who love all things electronics. This is our book imprint. We don't have many titles yet, but that's mostly because we are picky about the books we publish: we only publish books we'd read ourselves.

To see other books by GadChicks, or to read the FREE (yes, Free!) online magazine, visit GadChick.com.

Introduction

You bought a Mac! Let me be the first to tell you, your day is about to get much, MUCH easier.

But before we get there, there's a bit of light house keeping. Yeah, yeah, yeah - that's all well and good, but when do you get to play with your new machine?

Mac's are great - they are powerful, streamlined and easy as heck to use - but your files? They're still on a PC, and, like it or not, you just spent 20+ years using Windows, so there are some adjustments to make.

Before you can show off your slick new Macbook Air or brag about how much faster your machine boots up or how you can find a file in, like, three seconds, you need to make the transition.

That's what we're about to do. The accessories. The Apps. The file transfer. In the pages that follow, you'll learn all the stuff that matters, none of the stuff that doesn't and be ready to flash that shiny new Apple logo at your local coffee shop with pride.

Chapter 1: What Exactly Is a Macbook *Air*?

For the sake of argument, let's say you *haven't* already bought or decided to buy a Macbook Air. You haven't dropped fifty pound hints on the doorstep of whoever's on big-gift duty.

Maybe you have an iPhone or an iPad and thought, damn this thing is slick, I wish it worked better with my computer...

And then a year or two passed, and your old laptop flashed its final blue screen of death (you know the one:)

```
A problem has been detected and windows has been shut down to prevent damage
to your computer.

The problem seems to be caused by the following file: SPCMDCON.SYS

PAGE_FAULT_IN_NONPAGED_AREA

If this is the first time you've seen this stop error screen,
restart your computer. If this screen appears again, follow
these steps:

Check to make sure any new hardware or software is properly installed.
If this is a new installation, ask your hardware or software manufacturer
for any windows updates you might need.

If problems continue, disable or remove any newly installed hardware
or software. Disable BIOS memory options such as caching or shadowing.
If you need to use Safe Mode to remove or disable components, restart
your computer, press F8 to select Advanced Startup Options, and then
select Safe Mode.

Technical information:

*** STOP: 0x00000050 (0xFD3094C2,0x00000001,0xFBFE7617,0x00000000)

*** SPCMDCON.SYS   Address FBFE7617 base at FBFE5000, Datestamp 3d6dd67c
```

Now, you're ready to take the leap, dump your PC and buy a Mac. A quick glance shows that the Macbook Air is the most affordable Mac on the market; it's sleek and sexy and it's got power to spare, so what exactly are you buying?

Macbook Air vs. Its Older Brethren

First, the Air. Here's what Apple tells us on their website:

> 11.6 or 13.3 Inch Screen
> 1.7/8 GHz dual core i5 or 2.0 GHz dual-core Intel Core i7 Processor
> Less than 3 pounds
> 4GB or 8GB memory
> Up to 512GB Flash Storage (entry = 128GB)
> 5-7 Hours of Battery Life
> Starts at $999

If that doesn't mean anything to you, here's the gist - the Air is the entry level laptop. It's smaller, lighter, and faster than the larger and pricier Macbook Pro but it's not as powerful.

Why? Because of three things.

1. **It's Smaller** - Apple invented the ultralight notebook years before the rest caught on, and the Air is the perfected version of their vision. It's sleek. It's light (like WEIGHT light), and it can fit in just about anything. It also comes in 11" or 13" variants, so you can match it to your needs accordingly.

2. **Storage** - The Air uses SSD storage. This is the same storage as your iPhone or iPad. It's fast, like really fast. You know how it takes 2-3 minutes for your battered old PC to startup? That's the old disc hard drive spinning to life. It can only spin so fast, so you're stuck waiting. An SSD doesn't spin. It just...works. And it's fast. Trade off? It's about a quarter the size of a comparable entry level disc drive. So, less space for stuff.

3. **Lower Cost -** Cut price, and you get a less powerful machine. So, little or no gaming, sketchy photo editing and a lot less multi-tasking.

Just to make sure you're on the right trail, here's a look at what those same specs look like on a Macbook Pro or desktop iMac:

Up to 15" Screen (Retina Display available)
Up to 2.7 GHz quad-core Intel i7 processor
3.5-5.6 pounds
Up to 16GB memory
Up to 1TB Storage (512 SSD)
7 Hours of Battery Life
Starts at $1199

If you want to take a closer look at each Mac model and their specs, here's Apple's official comparison page:

http://www.apple.com/why-mac/compare/notebooks.html

Choosing Your Machine

Is a Macbook Air right for you? It depends.

Do you need a light machine? A sleek, low profile machine that will work extremely fast for email, word processing, photo editing, syncing your iPhone or iPad, and getting some work done on the go?

Then yes, this is the machine for you. They're perfect for college students, traveling salespeople, writers, and anyone with limited space.

You fit the bill? Keep reading - it's time to dump your PC.

Chapter 2: Windows to Mac at a Glance

Now you *know* how good a Macbook Air is, and you're tired of the headaches that come with a Windows machine - so let's get to the good stuff!

Before that, I have one more tour stop. Like it or not, you've just committed to a HUGE change.

When you switch to Mac, you're getting a machine and the software that runs on it - what Apple calls OSX. OSX is the Apple equivalent of Windows, and it's incredibly intuitive.

But, since Windows is often NOT, it can be a bit of a learning curve when you make the jump between the two.

Here are a few key differences you'd better be ready for when you flip open your Macbook for the first time.

A Difference in Philosophies

Steve Jobs was a lot of things, but what he'll probably long be remembered for is design and presentation. Sleek, simple, straightforward and so easy your grandma could pick it up and use it - that's the Jobs philosophy.

So, OSX is effortless. You turn it on, and your desktop has a handful of icons at the bottom of the screen. Apps are called simply "Mail" and "Calendar". No fluff, no filler. Just simplicity and tools that work.

Windows, on the other hand, wants to do EVERYTHING. It is designed to run software in hundreds of formats, to interface with thousands of different hardware peripherals and, as a result, it's loaded with bugs, plagued by viruses and bogged down by slow load times, bloat-ware and frustratingly arcane error codes.

Sure, there are more software options for PC, and Windows is truly universal, but if you're not a computer programmer or gamer, you probably won't notice. What you WILL notice is that your new Mac just plumb works. Fewer virus risks, fewer crashes, fewer junky software tools - just a single centralized platform that looks terrific and works even better.

Native Apps

You probably noticed a *slight* difference in price when you bought your Mac. It's not cheap. A comparable Windows PC would probably be half the price, but before you join the chorus of self-hating Apple fans who groan with every lineup reboot, consider what you get that Windows users *don't.*

Apple wants its users to have an experience. When you turn on a Mac, you have everything you need to start computing right now. Windows, less so. Consider some of the native apps that come with a Macbook Air:

Mail

Slightly more powerful than the mobile version, Mail on a Mac quickly and easily accesses your mail account (Gmail, Yahoo! or other) and downloads, sorts and indexes your messages. Windows has no alternative, just a buggy free version of Outlook that shows ads.

Calendar

Again, the Calendar app is straightforward, but that's what's so exciting. It interfaces with iCloud, syncs with your mobile devices, sends notifications and can import from a web calendar, all on autopilot.

iPhoto

The only way you'll interface with photos going forward and now with Photostream, iPhoto is immensely powerful, lightning fast and easy to sync between Macs or mobile devices. Again, only Windows 8 has a comparable alternative.

Messenger

Send text messages, IMs or just chat with people from your Mac - very cool if you don't want to keep your phone out while working.

iMovie

Windows does have a built-in video editor, but the Mac version is significantly more powerful, especially since it's built around the 720p webcam and microphone integrated in your machine.

GarageBand

A lot of you won't use this, but it's still impressive. Record vocals, create podcasts, or compose music all from your laptop - oh, and it's free.

Facetime

Another tool that works seamlessly between mobile and desktop - just load your contacts and call for a quick video chat.

iTunes

If you're used to buggy, slow, and frustratingly crash-y iTunes on Windows, take a deep breath because it is SO much faster on a Mac and with integrated functions your PC keyboard and interface can't match.

A few of these you can get on a PC and some Microsoft equivalents are available, but only Apple gives you a COMPLETE package on day one.

Mail, calendar, and the iPhoto/iMovie combo in particular are powerful tools that you won't find on a Windows machine - at least not in such an easy to use format. GarageBand may be an add on, but it's unbelievable software if you record audio in any format.

Sharing

It's not easy to compare Windows and OSX right now - OSX just received a new update that turned it into a native sharing operating system. You can login to Facebook and Twitter from the OS and share quite literally anything you use. You can create and use an iCloud account to share data between your laptop and your phone or tablet. You can download other software that uses the same iCloud tools to sync your data. It's a sharing machine.

Apple was WAY behind in the cloud computing field, but like almost everything they do, when they decided it was time to make a change, they one upped their opponents across the board.

So, why is it hard to make comparisons? Because Windows 7 and Vista, the two previous versions of Windows (and probably what you are switching from) had almost nothing in the way of sharing options.

Windows 8 is different, so I'll be fair - the big MS is working to catch up - but if you bought a Windows 8 machine you probably wouldn't be reading this and frankly, the Windows 8 sharing tools just aren't that perfect. We'll wait and see how they do in growing their app store, but for now it's a little bleak.

Gaming

If there is one place that Windows will alway have an edge, it is in gaming. Nine in ten computers sold are PCs. If you were a game developer, which would you build for?

It seems pretty obvious when you think of it like that, but at the same time, Mac may be starting to catch up. No, AAA titles are not being developed for the Mac in real time, but powerful developers like Blizzard have long created versions of their games (Starcraft II, Diablo III, World of Warcraft) for both platforms, and the Game Center now syncs between Mac, iPad and iPhone, and Apple is flat out killing it in the mobile space when it comes to gaming.

So, will they catch up? They darned well might. Should you buy a Mac if you are a hardcore gamer? Only if it's your second machine.

Productivity

Hands down, you can't beat a Mac when it comes to productivity. These things are built to help you get things done.

Let me give you just one example.

Let's say you need to write a 1,000 word article about the mating habits of the Kookaburra. So, you whip out your Macbook Air, open four pages in Safari and save them all to your reading list. You then open a Pages file (the Mac equivalent of MS Word) and start writing.

Twenty minutes later, you get a call. Your kid just Technicolor yawned all over the gymnasium floor, and you need to take him home sick. You save your file to iCloud, pick up the kid and take him home, then put him to bed.

While he sleeps you whip out your iPad and open your reading list, jotting down notes in the Notes app about your friend the Kookaburra.

When he's finally asleep, you turn your Macbook back on, sync the notes and finish your article.

From start to finish it's seamless. Just login to every device with your iCloud account and everything shows up.

A Windows machine *can* do the same thing, but it's not easy. The hardware needs to be synced, drivers need to be installed, software needs to be checked and synced, and if you already own an iPhone or iPad, it's not any easier.

This is not to mention the dozens of non-Apple apps that are designed under the Apple aesthetic model to work perfectly between OSX and iOS.

Windows 8 Is More Like OSX

Let's be fair to Microsoft - the newest version of Windows isn't bad. Stripped down, significantly faster and with fewer bugs than I've ever seen in a PC operating system, it's as close to OSX as they've ever come with a Windows build.

But, it's still not OSX. It's years behind - Macs have been working seamlessly with mobile devices for years already. The apps have been fine tuned to near perfection. The Mac App Store has more than 200,000 apps in it. The apps are cheaper, universal and work perfectly on any Mountain Lion capable machine.

Windows? You can't guarantee any of that – and it's still Windows at its core.

Chapter 3: OSX Mountain Lion Basics

Goodbye Windows! Shut it down, put it away, forget about it (for now at least - you still need your files), and turn on your Macbook.

Let's take a tour of Mountain Lion.

Mountain Lion is the official name for OSX version 10.8. Since OSX was released a few years ago, each iteration has been given a new name. If you bought yours before July 2012, you have Lion. A year or two before that, you might have had Snow Leopard.

But, Mountain Lion is the most recent release and so our tour will be in that OS.

This is your first Mac, so I'm going to roll things back to basics. Yes, this stuff is pretty straightforward, and yes you probably already figured most of it out, but hey, you never know what you might have missed.

Let's go!

The First Boot Up

Apple is famous for their product introductions. Flip the lid and hit the power button and you're greeted with the white screen, Mac jingle and a series of questions about you, your password, Wi-Fi network and iCloud login.

To be perfectly honest, Apple has made this more or less newbie proof - just answer their questions and follow the prompts. In less than 5 minutes, you'll be at the home screen.

The Home Screen

When you turn on a Windows machine for the first time, it's not this pretty. Why? Because not only do you have no idea what to do next, but there are dozens of bloat ware programs stuffed on your startup menu by the manufacturer.

Lucky for us Apple is the manufacturer this time, and they don't need to bloat the start menu (which we don't even have!)

So, when you finish the signup menus, this is what you'll see:

Let's run through each real quick:

Finder

Launchpad

Mission Control

App Store

Mail

Safari

iTunes

Calendar

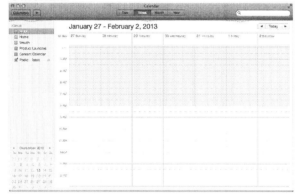

Notes

iPhoto

(source: Apple.com)

Preferences

Messenger

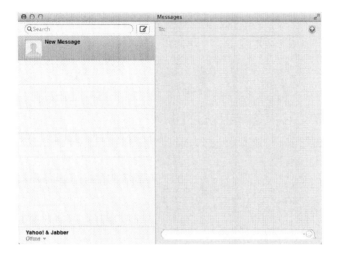

There are more apps of course - dozens of tools that come with a Mac out of the box, ready to work, but these are the ones you'll see the moment you turn it on. Make sure you are logged into your iCloud and iTunes accounts and you'll be instantly connected to all of your stuff.

Launching Apps

Want to launch an app? Easy. Just click on one from the home bar and it will open. Of course, nothing is instant. It takes between 2 and 10 seconds for an app to start, often it will bounce around until it does. Don't click it more than once - you'll only slow the process down.

Once it's running, there is a little white dot at the base of the dock to show you it's running in the background:

One HUGE difference between OSX and Windows is that, just because you can't see something running doesn't mean it's not. There are three places your Apps can disappear to if they're not on your screen:

1. The Dock

If the light is on, the app is open. To permanently close it, right click on the app and choose "Quit". For speed of shutdown, you might want to do this to any power hungry apps before you turn your computer off.

Apps like iTunes will keep playing music in the background when you close them, but will shut down completely when you "Quit" them.

2. The Task Bar

The Task Bar is at the top of your screen to the left of the date and time.

Anything that is SUPPOSED to run all the time goes up here. Things like Evernote, Dropbox, Bluetooth connections, your Wi-Fi network, and a bunch of other apps I'll show you soon go here.

These are notable because they will run silently and out of the way. They also happen to devour battery, so if you're unplugged consider right-clicking and quitting any that are not 100% necessary.

3. A New Space

Click on the Mission Control icon on your home bar:

This shows everything that is actively open right now. All of your apps that have data to display (a spreadsheet, iTunes, Safari windows, etc.) PLUS all of your Spaces.

A Space is a totally separate workspace on your desktop. Each space can contain different apps and make organizing your space MUCH easier.

When you turn on your Mac, it has two by default. If you click the little arrow at the top right of any app:

It will automatically go full screen and create a new space. But, you can also manually create new spaces and drop apps into them.

Keep your fun stuff separate from your work stuff. Separate your communication tools from each other or simply organize a boat load of research you're sorting through.

Installing New Apps

Apple has always been the company that protects your machine. No viruses, no blue screens, no random crashing.

And one way they do this is through strict quality control of software. If you use the officially recommended tools provided by Apple to download software, everything will be hunky dory. They test it; they require updates from developers and they distribute.

This is the App Store - the centralized interface for downloading new apps from Apple. Of course, not all apps are in the App Store, and to protect you from possibly suspect apps (malware is increasingly a problem for Macs as they become more popular), there is a Gatekeeper tool that blocks you from installing anything that doesn't belong there.

So, do your research before you install non-Apple verified apps.

Transferring from Windows

You're not done yet!

You still have years' worth of data on your Windows PC. Photos, movies, documents, spreadsheets, and whatever else you've been up to - it's all on one machine and needs to get to the new one.

Your Mac has a Windows Migration Assistant - it can be buggy as all heck, depending on the current health of your PC, but if it works, it's a good solution.

If you want to use it, however, here's how:

- Connect both computers to the same network (Wi-Fi or Wired)
- Open the Migration Assistant in Spotlight
- Before you start, make sure you also install the Migration assistant on you PC. You can download it from **http://www.apple.com/migrate-to-mac**.
- Open the file on your PC and click "Continue"
- Close everything on your Mac and choose "From another PC"
- Ideally, the Mac will now see your PC and the same code should display on both computer screens. If it doesn't, try turning off your antivirus software or firewall (usually in Windows)
- Check the boxes on everything want to move. Keep in mind that the migration tool will migrate everything into a NEW profile, not an existing one.

Keep in mind that if you have a much larger hard drive on your PC, you probably need to pare down the list a bit, so it fits. If it works, it will take a few hours, and then you'll be set.

Now, this doesn't always work – PC wonkiness, Apple dislike of PC interfaces – who knows, but it doesn't always work.

One more thing to keep in mind – you can get the gurus at the Apple Store to do this *for you*. For $99, you get a year of in-store training and a free PC migration. Just bring in your old computer and one of the Mac Genius guys will handle the transfer. This is probably the easiest way to get it done – it just costs a bit more.

If migration doesn't work and you don't want to spend another $100, your best bet is to do it manually. Before you plant your face on your desk for a lovely long nap, here's what that actually means:

1. **Backup Media** - The truly tough stuff is media - music, movies, and photos. Get them all onto an external hard drive. A Macbook Air has limited space anyways, so you'll probably want to keep everything on there for now.

2. **Drop Everything Else into a Cloud Account** - Signup for Dropbox, Box.net or iCloud and then dump all of your documents and other pertinent stuff into the account. Once it's all been uploaded, you can sign in on your Macbook and wham! It's all there. Most cloud accounts only offer between 2GB and 5GB of free space, so you may need to pay if your library is jumbo sized, but it's worth the peace of mind having a cloud backup provides.

3. **Don't Toss Your Windows Machine (yet)** -
   Whatever you do, don't throw out your Windows
   machine until you're 100% sure you have
   everything. The last thing you want is to move and
   find out 2 months later you forgot to remove an
   essential file.

The Trackpad

I *hated* my trackpad.

It had been three days since I bought my last
Windows laptop and the corner of the trackpad didn't
seem to be working right. The cursor skittered all
over the screen whenever I bumped it, and the
scrolling bar on the right? A joke. And not even a
funny one.

So, when I bought a Macbook some years later, you
won't blame me for buying a mouse to go with it, not
even thinking the trackpad was an option.

I should have placed greater trust in Apple because
the trackpad on the Macbook Air is the *only* one
you'll ever truly need.

But it's different, so first, some instructions.

Your trackpad is like your phone.

One finger moves the cursor - simple enough. Two
fingers moves the scroll bar - very cool, right? Three
fingers moves the entire screen - switching between

workspaces. Click with one finger, normal mouse click. Click with two fingers, right click. So, you can see the trackpad is actually USEFUL - not something you're used to, but impressive nonetheless.

Social Integration

Like it or not, and I know some of you may not, your computer is a conduit to social media the same as your phone.

It didn't used to be like this, not even for Apple. But, today when you buy a Macbook Air and turn it on for the first time, you log into your Facebook and Twitter accounts the same as you do your iCloud and iTunes accounts.

If you decide NOT to do this at startup or if you did without thinking and are eager to remove it, here's what to do.

Open preferences - the gear boxy looking icon on your home bar.

Now, open Mail, Contacts & Calendars. In here, you'll find as list of all your attached accounts.

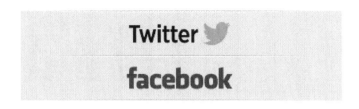

If you have a Facebook or Twitter account attached, delete it by hitting the "-" button on the bottom left.

If you want to add a new one, just click the appropriate account, login and start sharing.

Sharing is as easy on your laptop as on on your phone. You can share a photo straight from iPhoto, send something straight out of Safari or share a file or link from your desktop. Just click the familiar "send" icon:

👓 **Add to Reading List**

📖 **Add Bookmark**

📧 **Email this Page**

💬 **Message**

🐦 **Twitter**

f **Facebook**

And choose the account you want to send to. Voila, you've just shared to Twitter or Facebook.

Finding Your Files

Opinions vary on this one - some people dig the Mac's file system. Others find it slow and cumbersome.

You have a Macbook Air which means it's lightning fast, and if you learn to use the search functions right, everything is at your fingertips.

Of course, using it "right" is subjective, so let's take a quick look.

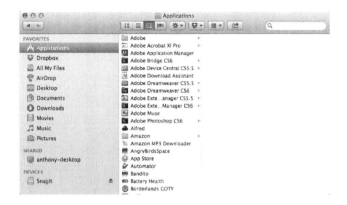

This is Finder. It is your friend. If there is a Windows equivalent, it's Explorer. But, Finder is better than Explorer for a few dozen reasons.

To start, your Mac will instantly (well, not instantly, but eventually) index all of your files. If you filled your hard drive to the brim, it would take a day or two to index everything, just for reference.

Anyways, it indexes your files so that when you search for something, it instantly (really this time), pulls up a list of matches. No lag time, no waiting - just a laundry list of possible matches.

Better yet, there are third party apps that make the search process faster, more efficient and easier to use. More on that in a bit.

This is the spotlight tool. So, if you need to do a quick search, you press CMD+Space, and it pops up. Type in your query and search, then voila, results.

Does it always work perfectly? No. It has a nasty habit of prioritizing results in funny ways (recent files, for example take precedent, even if older ones have exact matches in the filename).

But, it works a lot better than Windows Explorer, and for 99% of the people reading this, you'll be able to quickly and easily find your files.

The main problem you'll notice with this is that it is not conducive to organizing your files. You don't need to to be able to find them, which is worthless if you have a lot of files, so I HIGHLY recommend you go through and create folders, etc. But that's more a matter of your organizational preferences.

One more thing - this is iCloud. Every Apple account
has an iCloud storage space of 5GB. You can upgrade
it for the following:

If you don't have a cloud storage account, this is a
pretty good deal. If you do, with Dropbox or Box or
any of the others, it's probably not necessary.

You can save a lot of things to iCloud, usually
directly through the app, so you can't create folders,
store things in your own format, etc. BUT you *can*
access them on mobile devices FROM the apps,
which is pretty slick.

Tips for Macbook Zen Mastery

Okay, okay, you're saying, I get it already. But what about....

The cool thing about a Mac (or frustrating thing depending on how quickly it happens) is that everything you see is surface level.

The slick apps, seamless animation and super sexy aluminum body are all eye candy - your new computer is also a BEAST under the hood. It can do incredible things, but only if you know how to tap its inner workhorse.

In this section, we're going to dig deeper and take a look at all the groovy things you can do with a Mac, from supercharging your battery life to running Windows apps on it (God forbid you need to).

Everything you'll *actually* want to do? That's in this section:

Data, Storage and Space

The one thing you've likely compromised on in buying a Macbook Air is the amount of available storage. It's smaller. Entry level Airs have 128GB of storage and larger ones have 512GB.

Five years ago that would have been great. Today, not so much.

For reference, that's about 40 and 80 hours of video respectively. Two seasons of Law and Order and you're toast.

Fortunately, there are a lot of tools in Mountain Lion you can use to save space and streamline operations.

1. Storing to an External Hard Drive

Your first option is to save to an external drive. You can get a Time Capsule USB backup from Apple or a standard USB desktop drive. Any drive will work - it just needs to be formatted for compatibility with your Mac and nine times out of ten; it will tell you when this is necessary.

Why is this in the advanced section? Because you can setup Time Machine to automatically backup your files to an external drive.

This is the icon for the Time Machine, and it will remain in the menu bar, even when off. Click on the Preferences option to open this menu:

Then turn it "On" and choose which external hard drive to use. Then, voila, you have a time machine backup of your computer. If something happens to your hard drive, and if you keep your machine long enough, it certainly will, you can quickly and easily swap in the old save.

2. Using iCloud

Apple's cloud service isn't as robust as something like Dropbox or Box.net. It doesn't support your own folder structures and is tied to specific apps, so it's only useful for backing up things like your documents, spreadsheets and keynote presentations. It's also perfect for photos, notes, contacts, and Safari data. Certain apps will work with it as well, but how they do is up to the third party developer that creates those apps.

3. Cutting Down on Space Used

Okay, so there are a couple ways to back up your data and keep it on an external drive. But how do you keep your machine from filling up in the first place?

Here are a few quick tips to keep your hard drive for boiling over in the first few weeks.

Webmail

The Mail app is great - it's fast and opens automatically when you turn your machine on, but it's also a vampire - sucking the free storage away from your machine for no good reason.

Webmail interfaces are more powerful than ever before, and they have storage limits well above and beyond what you will ever fill up. Why store 10GB of mail on your machine when Google will do it for you?

If you truly hate using a web-based email client or if you need to be sure you have access to your mail at all times, consider changing to a POP connection. This will show the messages on the server, not on your computer.

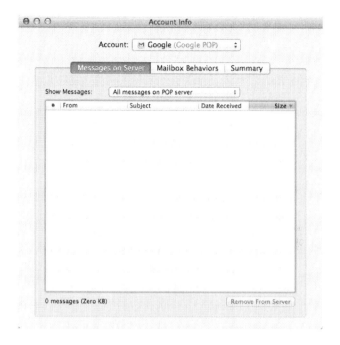

You'll need to change the actual configurations in Mail to do this, but it will save a ton of space. Be warned that it is slower than IMAP and you can't search your messages when disconnected from the Internet, but you'll get that space back.

Turn Off Auto Backups

By default, auto backups are done to an external hard drive, but there are some ways that Mac uses up space for backups.

Even with auto backups off, it will store some data on your main hard drive for document restoration. These are called local backups, and they occur whenever you create or delete a humongous chunk of data.

Great if you accidentally delete something - horrible if you're trying to save space on a small SSD hard drive.

Before you do ANYTHING, know that you'll be using Terminal - the tool that allows you to actually communicate with the command-line code of your machine. If anything I show you next looks like Greek, hold off. An Apple Store Genius can help you better than this book. Now, for the fix.

With that terrifying warning out of the way, this isn't actually too hard. Just open Terminal (search in Spotlight):

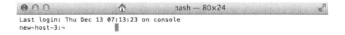

Now, type the following:

sudo tmutil disablelocal

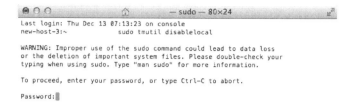

```
Last login: Thu Dec 13 07:13:23 on console
new-host-3:~          sudo tmutil disablelocal

WARNING: Improper use of the sudo command could lead to data loss
or the deletion of important system files. Please double-check your
typing when using sudo. Type "man sudo" for more information.

To proceed, enter your password, or type Ctrl-C to abort.

Password:
```

You'll need to enter your admin password to verify. If you ever decide to change back, use the following

sudo tmutil enablelocal

Of course, if you do this, make sure you keep close track of your data and backup crucial documents regularly - your Mac isn't doing it for you any longer.

Stream Audio and Video

The last 15 months have been a boon for Mac owners with limited space. Apple is streaming!

If you have a massive iTunes collection that instantly fills half your hard drive upon migration, this is a MUST.

Open iTunes, then go to the Store menu on the file tab at the top:

Store	Window	Help	
Back			⌘[
Forward			⌘]
Home			⇧⌘H
Reload Page			⌘R
Turn On iTunes Match			
Turn On Genius			
Authorize This Computer...			
Deauthorize This Computer...			
Deauthorize Audible Account...			
Sign In...			
Create Apple ID...			
Check for Available Downloads...			

Now, choose to "Turn on iTunes Match". Keep in mind that this service DOES cost money - $24.99 per year - but it's well worth it. Alternatives include Amazon Cloud Player, Google Play Music, RealPlayer, Napster and Spotify. All offer some variation of the same service - cloud based music.

I recommend Apple's if only because it works inside of iTunes, syncs with your Apple ID (so you can use it on your mobile devices) and the audio quality is top tier.

Video streaming isn't quite on the same level yet, but it's coming. If you do download a lot of movies to your computer, put them on an external drive as soon as you watch them. It wouldn't take long to fill up a Macbook Air drive with HD movies.

Use CCleaner

It's one of my top App recommendations, and it's free, so you have literally ZERO reason not to download it.

Get to the App Store, download CCleaner and set it to run every 1-2 weeks. When it does, old files, Safari data and unneeded info will be wiped from your drive. Pesky leftover Trash data (because who remembers to empty their trash?) will be wiped, as well.

CCleaner has quite a few options, but to keep your drive as clear as possible uninstall any old apps you don't use with the Tools menu:

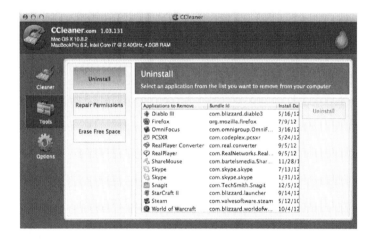

Cool Tools in Mountain Lion

Most of the basic stuff, I covered in the last section - your Mission Control and Launchpad, iLife apps, etc.

But, there are a few other very sophisticated tools built into Mountain Lion that can supercharge your productivity, and I want to make sure you know where to find them.

Dictation

Your phone (and/or iPad) has a dictation function. Press the little microphone on your keyboard like so:

And you can dictate. It's moderately accurate (when in a quiet room), but it's a little slow - about the speed of Siri.

Mountain Lion, however, has a much faster, MUCH more useful dictation tool. Of course, there are limitations, as well.

First, you can only dictate for 30 seconds at a time. After 30 seconds, it shuts off and processes. This is because it uses an external Apple server to transliterate speech to text. It also takes 2-3 seconds to process each 30 second burst of speech, and of course, it's never quite 100% accurate.

To use it, simply double-tap the 'fn' (function) key and wait for the sound to announce it is ready, speak into your microphone and then press enter. Voila, speech to text.

Some additional tools here:

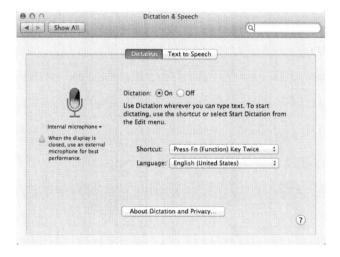

You can turn dictation on or off as you please - there is no real benefit to turning it off, but if you never use it, this is an option. You can also change the key used to start the function and right now, Dictation supports 8 languages, most of them with multiple dialects, so it's not just for English.

Another option, should you wish your computer to talk to YOU, is to turn on Text to Speech as shown above. Simply check the "Speak selected text when the key is pressed" box, and you can use the selected macro to have the computer read whatever you type back. Does it sound good? Not really, but it can be extremely effective if you are in a hurry.

Quick and Dirty Shortcuts

One reason the Mac has been so popular with designers and coders is that it's built to hack - shortcuts, macros, automations. It's all there. Here are a few built in shortcuts to make your life easier:

* **Duplicate Fast** - Highlight a file or folder and press COMMAND+D to duplicate it
* **Accessibility** - Open Universal Access with COMMAND+OPTION+F5

* **Notifications** - The notifications bar is in the top right corner - to open it without having to click the bar, slide two fingers from right to left
* **Keyboard Shortcuts** - Forgot where to go for Mission Control? Just press F3 and it will pop up automatically. F4 for Launchpad.
* **App Switching** – Rapidly switch between apps by pressing COMMAND+TAB. You can scroll through apps if you hold down COMMAND and keep pressing TAB.
* **Screenshots** – Your Mac has a built-in screenshot tool. Just press COMMAND-SHIFT-3 and it will save a screenshot of the current screen to your desktop. Press COMMAND-SHIFT-4 to choose which part of the screen to capture.
* **Empty Trash** – In case you forget or don't feel like right clicking the trash can, press COMMAND-SHIFT-DELETE to empty your trash.
* **Dashboard** – Check out your dashboard widget dock by pressing COMMAND-PLUS(+). Cycle through your widgets with the arrow button while holding COMMAND.
* **Spaces** – You can combine all spaces into a single space by entering Mission Control and pressing C.

This is just a quick selection of commands I find useful – here is a more comprehensive list courtesy of DanRodney - **http://www.danrodney.com/mac/**

Extending Battery Life

Next on our tour of vital but hidden Mountain Lion functions is battery life. It's not flashy, but it's noteworthy because the last thing you want is your computer dying after three hours when at the airport, especially when you're expecting the 5-7 hours Apple promised you.

In fact, one of the most common complaints I hear about new Macs is the underwhelming battery performance. Rest assured - we can fix it. That battery WILL last as long as it's supposed to (or longer!) - it just needs some tinkering.

Before starting with this, check out this nifty app:

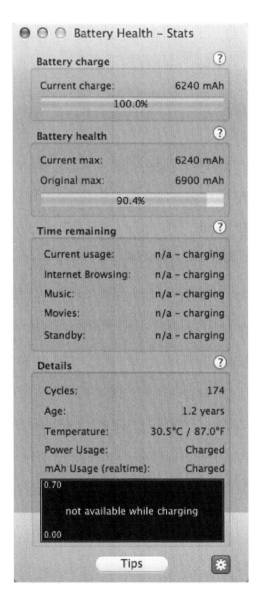

It's called Battery Health and it's free in the App
Store. It shows you current charge, overall health

(capacity) and how long it will last doing a number of different tasks. All very cool, and exceptionally helpful when deciding what to turn off and what to leave on.

Energy Saver

Energy saver settings on the Macbook Air are pretty limited. You can change when it goes to sleep, when the display turns off and whether the display dims or not:

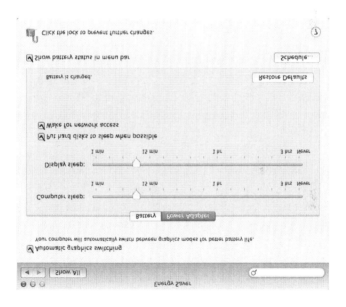

Set the sleep times for as low as possible without annoying you when unplugged and check the box at the top that says "Automatic Graphic Switching" as this will bump battery life between 5-15%.

Managing Bluetooth and Wireless

Number one on your to do list is Wireless and Bluetooth. Both are located in the menu bar here:

To turn either off, simply click the icon and select "off". This is especially noteworthy for Bluetooth which can truly drain battery, especially if you have an active Bluetooth device in your carrying case and it's trying to connect.

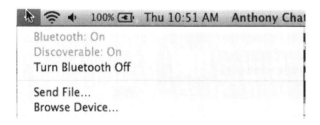

Now, your Air is rated for battery use with Wi-Fi ON, but it'll run even better with it off, so whenever you don't need Internet, turn it off. Even if you're not connected, the wireless card is constantly seeking and trying to connect to any nearby options.

App Dock Management

The home bar or App Dock at the bottom of your screen is filled with often used apps, and because most of them stay open, even when you're not using them, it can drain your battery fast.

This is what an app dock looks like after turning on the machine. Now, look at this:

That's after a couple hours of checking email, surfing the web, taking notes and writing articles. But, here's Mission Control:

Empty. So, there's nothing running, right?

Not so fast. You see those little white lights beneath the apps - that means it's still in memory. No, you don't have any files open, but the App is still sitting there ready to be used. That eats batter life.

If you're going to leave Apps open, keep it to a minimum - Skype, Mail, Calendar, Safari - close battery hogs like Evernote, iPhoto, iTunes, and anything third party.

Screen Brightness Impact

You know it matters, but do you know how much?

The brightness of your screen is the single biggest battery drain on your machine, besides maybe video streaming and gaming. So, how do you change it?

OSX uses the webcam to dynamically change brightness to match your environment. So, bright natural light means it turns up. Low light and it turns down. Very useful for short use, but for prolonged use when the battery needs to last? It can drain it fast.

To turn the brightness down and keep it down, open the Brightness Preferences (search for Displays or open in Preferences):

Now, uncheck the "Automatically adjust brightness" box and set the brightness to the lowest point where you can still see comfortably.

Time Machine

OSX has a nifty tool called Time Machine. Here's a look at me working on this document:

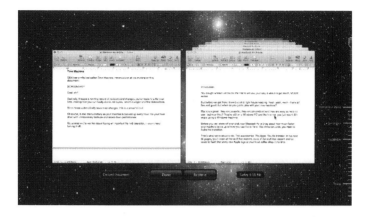

Cool, eh?

Basically, it keeps a running record of revisions and changes you've made to a file over time, making it so you can easily check old copies, revert changes and find deleted text.

Since Macs automatically save most changes, this is a powerful tool.

Of course, it also drains battery as your machine is backed up every hour, fills your hard drive with unnecessary backups and slows down performance.

So, unless you're worried about losing an valuable file mid-operation, I recommend turning it off.

Go to Preferences, then click on Time Machine like so:

And click the "Off" button.

You can also turn it back on if you want to run backups for any period of time, such as when plugged into a workstation at home or in the office.

If you leave it on and want to access those backups, click the "File" menu for whatever App you're using:

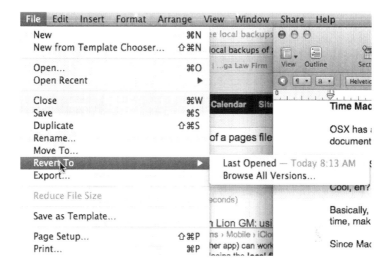

Go to "Revert to" and choose "All Versions" - then you'll see the full list of possible local backups you can access.

Turnoff Indexing

Another seriously cool feature of Macs that also happens to eat battery life AND storage space is indexing.

Whenever you put new files on your machine, move something around or save a large volume of pictures or music files, they get indexed.

This makes it possible for you to search for them in Finder super-fast. It also eats battery life because your machine is ALWAYS indexing. Exhaustingly so.

To turn it off, open Terminal.

Now enter the following command:

sudo mdutil -a -i off

To turn it back on, enter:

sudo mdutil -a -i on

Remember, only use Terminal if you're 100% confident that you can do it without messing anything up.

Another thing you can do if you're worried about slow performance due to indexing is reset your PRAM.

Don't worry about what PRAM actually does - just know that a quick reset will often speed up the computer at startup.

- Turn off your computer
- Hold down COMMAND+OPTION-P-R and turn on your computer
- Keep holding them down until the computer restarts and you hear the startup sound the SECOND time
- Release the keys and let your computer boot normally

This should ALWAYS make the Air bootup faster – it may not solve all your problems, but it's a good start.

Mission Control 101

Mission Control and Launchpad are extremely unassuming at first glance. Heck, Launchpad looks like a big version of your iPhone's home screen. But, there's a lot under the surface. Here are a few things you should know.

Search in Launchpad

Can't remember what app you need? Or have dozens and no idea where the one you need is? Do a quick search.

Yes, you can do a search from the desktop through Spotlight (COMMAND+SPACE) or with a tool like Alfred or Quicksilver, but the search bar in Launchpad is there if you forget:

Also, while in Launchpad, you can organize your apps the same as you would in iOS by dragging them into folders:

The same trick works for widgets on your Dashboard (for those that use the Dashboard)

Creating New Spaces

Do me a favor and click on Mission Control:

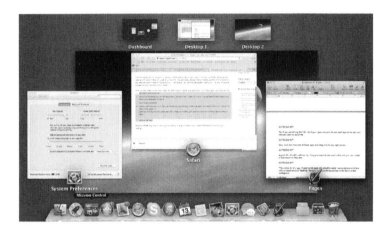

You'll see something like this - all of your open documents and apps layered so you can choose which to switch to.

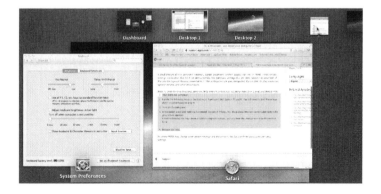

Now, click and hold one of those apps and drag it to the top right corner:

A giant PLUS button will pop up. Drag your app into the plus button and you can create a new space for that app.

This works for any app, though some apps will actually create new screens and others will just duplicate your desktop.

For any app with the following button in the top right corner, simply press escape to exit full screen:

But for other apps that you create a new workspace for, you can delete your extra workspace by returning to mission control and clicking on the extra workspace at the top:

Now, press the "X" to close it.

Voila, the incredible growing and shrinking desktop.

Chapter 4: Running Windows on a Mac

Why the heck would you want to do that?

Well, there are good reasons. Yes, installing Windows on a perfectly good Mac sound insane, but there may be times when you want or even NEED a piece of software only available for Windows. It happens a lot.

So, if you don't have a Windows machine handy, you'll need a workaround. Fortunately, there are a few options. Unfortunately, they are all slightly complicated.

Bootcamp

To start, there is Bootcamp, supplied by Apple to install Windows on your Mac. You will need a Windows installation disc or USB stick (and since Microsoft doesn't make these, you'll need to make one).

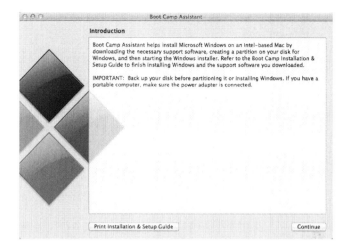

To install Windows, OSX will partition your hard drive, which means even less space, but if you're only installing to run a few select programs, it won't need *that* much space.

It's pretty straightforward, once you get the disc and an external DVD drive to read it, but keep in mind that Bootcamp Windows installations never run quite right, and not all software will run on your Air, even with Bootcamp there.

Software on Windows

There is a tool called Wine that allows your Mac to read slightly altered Windows software. Here's how it works.

Someone takes a Windows program they REALLY want on their Mac. They then write a series of commands that *teach* your Mac how to read that file, with the help of an external program like Wine.

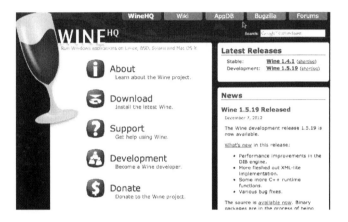

You then download Wine, the extra bit of code AND the Windows program and run all three at once. In an ideal world, it runs smoothly, and you have Windows software on your Mac.

In reality, it will probably be buggy and slow. Great for small programs that you need to use real quick to edit a file, but horrible for larger tools or software you just don't want to repurchase in Mac format.

You can download Wine from
http://www.winehq.com

VMWare

There are a few third party tools as well that install a "virtual machine" on your Mac. This is essentially the same thing as Bootcamp, but a little cooler. Instead of creating a partition you boot into when you turn your computer on, VMWare (or Parallels, a comparable tool, allows you to launch Windows FROM your Mac's home screen.

It will load in the background, and you can then run Windows in a separate window or even a new workspace.

On a Macbook Air, it's not the smoothest process, but as far as performance goes, it's probably your best bet.

The downside of course is that VMWare and similar tools are pricey, so it's not terribly an option unless you NEED it.

Change Your Dock

This is where you can set things like the color of tabs and windows, your desktop background, dock settings and more. In fact, before we move on, let's take a closer look at dock settings.

First, there is size. Make your icons smaller or bigger as you see fit. They will automatically change based on the number of open apps, but for starters it's good to have options.

You can also create a cool magnification effect when you mouse over an app like so:

Even more importantly, you can decide where you
want your dock. It's on the bottom by default, but if it
bothers you there the left and right are also options.

Chapter 5: Troubleshooting

Macs are not impervious to problems. There are thousands of techies in blue shirts bemoaning the fact that, deservedly so, the Mac has a reputation for being virus-proof and more stable than a PC.

It is, but it's still a computer and computers crash.

So, before you run to an Apple Store Genius Bar cradling your Air to your chest like a wounded bird, consider some of these potential problems and their solutions.

Force Quitting

The rainbow wheel. Get used to this - it means your computer is stuck, or frozen, or just downright tired.

The cool (or awful, depending on your perspective) thing about Macs is that they generally run perfectly up until the point you push them too far. So, you can keep opening new apps, running dozens of things at once and then....nothing.

When an app freezes, refuses to close or starts acting funny, we use force quit.

Force Quit is the Apple equivalent of control-alt-delete on a Windows computer. There are three ways to force quit.

1. **Click on the App Menu and Choose Force Quit** - Top right corner, whatever app you're running, click Force Quit from the menu. Not often an option because...well, it's frozen.

2. **Right Click on Icon** - Click the icon in your dock and choose "Force Quit". This works when the first option doesn't more often than not. Might take some time to get there, but take a deep breath and wait; it'll come up.

3. **Keyboard Shortcut** - Finally, there's the keyboard shortcut. Just type COMMAND-OPTION-ESCAPE and you'll get a menu of all open apps that can be Force Quit.

Apple doesn't give you the courtesy of pointing out which app is pissing you off, but you can usually figure it out pretty quick, and because your apps almost constantly auto-save it's unlikely you'll lose any data.

It's Running So...Slooow!

Slow computers are not fun. You buy your new Air, bring it home and enjoy the zippy, almost instant interface. Then it starts to bog down. Here are some quick fixes if this happens to you:

Spotlight Search

Remember, your computer is indexing whenever you dump a pile of new files on the hard drive. The Air does this better than a Pro or iMac, but it's still pretty slow. Click the Spotlight icon in the top right to see if this is the problem:

If it is, you'll just have to wait...or turn off indexing, though that can make finding your files a nightmare.

Running Out of Space

If you start to run out of space, which is pretty likely with a Macbook Air SSD, you'll need to clear some space. To check, open Finder:

Click on the View Menu and then Show Status Bar:

View	Go	Window	Help

as Icons	⌘1
as List	⌘2
✓ as Columns	⌘3
as Cover Flow	⌘4
Clean Up	
Clean Up By	▶
Arrange By	▶
Show Path Bar	
Show Status Bar	⌘/
Hide Sidebar	⌥⌘S
Hide Toolbar	⌥⌘T
Customize Toolbar...	
Show View Options	⌘J

You'll see available space at the bottom now:

112 items, 390.88 GB available

Less than 10GB and you're running out of space.
Time to clear things out. Run CCleaner, remove files
you know you don't need, move media to a backup
drive and restart your computer. That should fix it.

Memory

Your computer has memory or RAM that runs programs. Not enough available and everything slows down, not just the new apps you try to open.

An Air has less trouble with this than a Pro, but it's still a hefty slowdown problem. To check, open the Activity Monitor (do a search in Spotlight or Alfred):

Click on System Memory:

Now, check to see what is free.

If the Pie Chart on the right shows no green, you're in a bad shape.

To clear up space, start by closing apps you don't need. If you have 20 tabs open in Safari or Chrome, CLOSE THEM - that's the #1 memory hog on your machine. Then recheck your Activity Monitor to see if the problem is solved.

Of course, if you run out of RAM entirely, you can talk to someone at the Genius Bar and see if an upgrade is possible. For most Air models, it is not, but there are some exceptions, including some external upgrades.

For the most part, this shouldn't happen, so if memory is becoming a massive problem, something might be failing - in which case your Applecare will cover the repairs.

Five More Quick Tips for Faster Operation

Still not fast enough? Here are five more tips to crank up the speed on your machine:

1. Fewer Login Items

When you turn your machine on, how many icons appear in the menutab? The more you have, the slower it starts up, so remove a few. Open System Preferences and choose Users & Groups:

Then go to Login Items:

Uncheck everything you'd rather not have on.

2. Clear Your Desktop

Get rid of the icons on your desktop. You don't need
them - that's what Spotlight is for. Keep it to less than
20 or so icons and the speed boost will be noticeable.

3. Updates

The App Store will tell you when an update is
available - download it! If your machine needs an
update, there's a reason. This goes double for any
Mountain Lion or Safari updates.

It can take a few minutes to do the update, but it's worthwhile to get it done NOW, not later.

4. Reinstall OSX

It's not fun, but sometimes, a fresh install is the best way to speed up your machine. The odds are that you DON'T need to do this with a brand new Macbook. Try everything else in this section first, and possibly see a Genius Bar tech before rebooting.

But, if you keep having trouble, nothing is running, and your memory and hard drive are in good shape, a reboot might be your best bet.

To do so, download a copy of Mountain Lion in the App Store (if it's not already in your Launchpad):

Then start the App and choose "Continue" from the menu:

OS X Mountain Lion

To set up the installation of OS X 10.8 Mountain Lion, click Continue.

Continue

Make sure all of your data is backed up first of course - this is where turning on Time Capsule can certainly come in handy.

5. Turn Off Thumbnails

When you open Finder and click on an icon, it will show you a preview and thumbnail of the file:

Name	Macbook Air Article
Kind	Microsoft Word 97...
Size	174 KB
Created	Today 9:18 AM
Modified	Today 9:18 AM
Last opened	Today 11:14 AM

It's tremendously cool, right?

Of course like all tremendously cool features, it eats battery, storage space and CPU power when it's being used.

To turn it off, open Finder, then click on the View tab in the File Menu Bar:

View	Go	Window	Help
as Icons			⌘1
as List			⌘2
✓ as Columns			⌘3
as Cover Flow			⌘4
Clean Up			
Clean Up By			▶
Arrange By			▶
Show Path Bar			
Hide Status Bar			⌘/
Hide Sidebar			⌥⌘S
Hide Toolbar			⌥⌘T
Customize Toolbar...			
Hide View Options			⌘J

Then choose View Options and Uncheck "Show Icon Preview. That should provide a bit of a boost when in Finder.

Recovery Mode

Mountain Lion has a nifty invisible partition for recovery - if something breaks on your hard drive, you can boot to the recovery partition and restore the rest of your machine.

I sincerely hope you NEVER need this, but if you do, here's a quick primer on how to use it.

Restart your machine and hold down COMMAND+R. You should see a window that says "OS X Utilities".

If this doesn't work, press OPTION when restarting and the Startup Manager pops up.

Just choose the Recovery Drive from here and you're set.

From here, you have a few options:

If you have a Time Machine backup you can boot from it, or you can choose to just Reinstall OSX from scratch. There is also a Disk Utility to make some basic changes or run troubleshooters, though I don't recommend you use this unless you already know your way around (in which case, why are you reading this?)

Of course, if your hard drive has quite literally bitten the dust and you need to get it swapped out, the recovery mode won't work - you'll need to send it back to Apple.

Keep in mind too that Mountain Lion (on mid-2011 or later Macbook Airs) allows you to do an Internet Recovery. This doesn't require a partition - you can simply download the necessary files while IN recovery mode and reboot your machine.

To enter Internet Recovery at startup, press COMMAND+OPTION+R and hold it down until it boots.

Chapter 6: Must have Mac Apps

Apple has mastered the art of software delivery. The App Store is as easy as it gets. Point, click, download and use.

But, it's filled with its fair share of clunkers, so you want to be sure you pick only the crème de la crème of apps - here are a few of my favorites:

Evernote

Free – App Store

If you don't have Evernote on your phone or tablet, get it now, then download it for your Macbook Air. It doesn't get easier to take notes, sync them between multiple devices and organize your life. Plus, it is 100%, unequivocally free!

Pages/Numbers/Keynote

$19.99 Each – App Store

I've jammed these into one tidy package for good
reason, but you can buy them alone if you like. This
is the iWork suite - Apple's answer to the clunky,
overpriced MS Office (seriously, it runs...less than
optimal on a Mac). Do they have the same functions
as Microsoft's super tools? Not really, but for 90% of
this book's readers, they'll get the job done, plus they
feature iCloud support and all three are available on
iOS.

Skype

Skype for Mac

There's so much you can do with Skype – share a
bedtime story, host a meeting or take a language class

Here's just a few of the great things you can do

✓ Free Skype to Skype calls
✓ Low cost calls and text messages to mobiles and
   landlines
✓ Video call on Skype and Facebook
✓ Free instant messages to your friends, family and
   colleagues

All you need to get started is Mac OS X v10.5.8
(Leopard) or above, a webcam for video calls and a
microphone

Get Skype for Mac ⬇

System requirements

Free - **http://beta.skype.com/en/download-skype/skype-for-computer/**

Free, Mac-friendly and also available on your mobile
devices, Skype is a must have for any computer, but
especially your Mac. With an exceptional webcam
and microphone, superlight body and long battery
life, this is a terrific way to stay in touch.

CCleaner

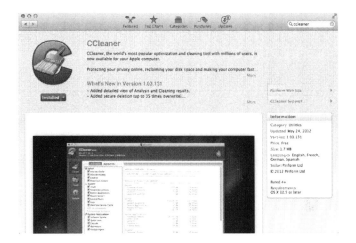

Free – App Store

Macs are still computers. They bloat with old files, slow down with fragmented hard drives, and they run out of space (especially the Air). That's where CCleaner comes in. This free utility takes a vacuum brush to your storage and memory, wiping away old files from your hard drive, opening up new space and making everything squeaky clean and faster. Run it every 2-3 weeks for optimal performance.

Dropbox (or other)

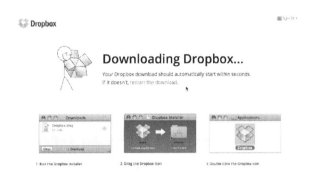

Free – **http://www.dropbox.com**

I don't have a personal preference, but the ONE thing you gave up by buying a Macbook Air is storage, so if you have a lot of files you need some kind of cloud storage account. Dropbox is the easiest to use, but there are others - Box.net, Amazon Cloud, Google Drive, and iCloud - pick your poison and start saving space.

Firefox/Chrome

Free – **http://www.getfirefox.com**

Don't get me wrong, I LOVE Safari, but when only 9% of computers are Macs and Safari isn't supported on Windows, webmasters tend to ignore it. So, a lot of sites, especially data intensive sites and backends such as Wordpress, don't run that swell in Safari, so get an alternative - I like Chrome for its speed, but Firefox is another brilliant one.

Things

$49.99 – App Store

Here's another one with a dozen options to choose from. I give you Things because it's simple, affordable and doesn't require $20+ apps for your phone and table. But others like Omnifocus are even more powerful and just as pretty. If you need a powerful, Mac-styled to do list Things is a fantastic place to start though.

Facebook Menutab

$1.99 (Free Version Available) – App Store

Despite deep Facebook integration, OSX still doesn't have a native application for viewing your Facebook posts and messages. Enter Facebook Menutab. The basic app is free; it sits in your menubar, and it tells you whenever a new message or notification pops up - very cool.

Alfred

$4.99 – App Store

Remember when I said third party apps could help you search your machine faster? Bingo - we have Alfred. By far the coolest and most efficient option for speedy hard drive searches, Alfred can instant launch any of your apps or files with a few keystrokes. Do yourself a favor and watch the tutorial when you download - this thing is MUCH more powerful than it appears on the surface.

RemoteMouse

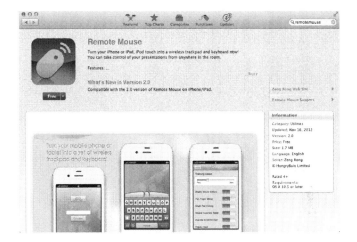

Free – App Store

Super handy for presentations or simply when you're tired of using the trackpad, RemoteMouse creates a Bluetooth link with your iPhone so you can use it as a mouse. That's it, but simple or not, it's immensely cool to do.

Reeder

$4.99 – App Store

If you follow a lot of blogs, or heck, even just a couple, this is a must. Instead of bookmarking and opening a dozen tabs every morning, Reeder will scour your RSS feed and display recent posts right on your desktop.

Day One

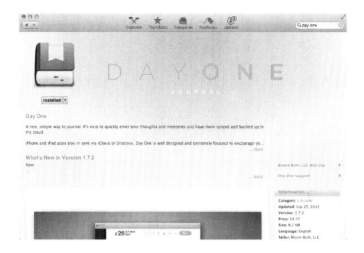

$4.99 – App Store

There are dozens of journaling apps in the App Store, but again, this is a Mac - so get the one that matches the rest of your stuff. This is my favorite for a number of reasons. to start, it's sleek and uncluttered. Second, it runs in the menu tab and will pop up at certain times each day reminding you to journal. Third, it has an iOS app so you can journal on your phone or tablet and save to iCloud.

Caffeine

Free – App Store

A big problem with laptops is that they tend to shut down if you walk away for a few seconds. Unlike Windows, OSX doesn't offer a native 'always on' mode, so you need an app. Caffeine sits in your menu bar and, when activated won't let your screen or hard drive shut down to save battery. A must when downloading a file, streaming video or going to the bathroom with a form open in Safari.

Hazel/Keyboard Maestro

$25 - http://www.noodlesoft.com/hazel.php

There are organizational tools, and then there is
Hazel. This thing is incredibly powerful, essentially
allowing you to define specific circumstances that
will organize, file and process files, photos and just
about anything else you have on your machine in just
seconds. Keyboard maestro is roughly the same thing,
but it does it through keyboard and mouse macros -
basically you can map pretty much any action on your
machine to a series of keystrokes to play music,

Quicksilver

Free – **http://qsapp.com**

Your Mac is going to have a lot of STUFF on it soon.
Music, apps, widgets, links, files - you name it and
there will be a folder overflowing with it in short
order. Spotlight and Mission Control are impressive,
but Quicksilver takes content management and, more
importantly, access to a new level. It's also free,
unlike Alfred and it's been around for a LONG time,
meaning it has been updated to the point of near
perfection.

PixelMator

$29.99 – App Store

If you're a designer, Photoshop is the Queen Bee of the photo editing world, but Pixelmator is a surprisingly powerful alternative for the Mac, and at 10% of the price, it's a steal. If you edit things sparingly or need a photo retouching tool, this is your best bet on a budget.

AppFresh

metaquark

AppFresh for Mac

AppFresh helps you to keep all applications, widgets, preference panes and application plugins installed on your Mac up to date. All from one place, easy to use and fully integrated into Mac OS X. AppFresh works by checking the excellent osx.iusethis.com for new versions and lets you download and install available updates easily.

⬇ Download v1.0   🛒 Buy Now $14.99

$14.99 – **http://metaquark.de/appfresh/**

Not everything on your Mac will go through the App Store, so a tool like AppFresh will provide you with a centralized, easy to use tool for updating apps instantly whenever an update comes in. Antivirus, App Store, Microsoft Updates and anything else you have on your machine will be done at once - super easy.

Avast!

Free - **http://www.avast.com/free-antivirus-mac**

So, there's a nasty rumor that Macs don't get viruses. Were that it was true. Macs get LESS viruses, but no computer is 100% safe from infection. Unauthorized apps, cleverly coded websites or unencoded WiFi networks can all create problems on your machine - so protect it with this free antivirus tool.

The Unarchiver

Free – App Store

Yes, OSX comes with a tool for opening zip files, but it only works on a small number of extensions. If you've ever gotten a file from a colleague or client that just wouldn't open, The Unarchiver will crack it.

Chapter 7: Best Accessories for Macbook Air

It's tempting to think you're done - the slick white box, the sleek brushed aluminum frame. It's a sexy package - but to genuinely get the most out of your new laptop you'll need a few things.

Do you need everything on this list? Probably not. Actually scratch that, almost certainly not.

But, different people have different needs, and these are my top 15 choices for Macbook Air accessories - the stuff that will truly milk your machine for all its worth. Here you go:

Magic Mouse

$69.99 -
**http://store.apple.com/us/product/MB829LL/A/ap
ple-magic-mouse**

Quite possibly the coolest mouse ever created - yes, it's pricey and yes your Air will work just fine with another Bluetooth or USB mouse, but none will ever be as cool as the Magic Mouse - multitouch, wireless and no buttons, it's that good.

Wireless Keyboard

$69.99 -
**http://store.apple.com/us/product/MC184LL/B/ap
ple-wireless-keyboard-english**

If you have a lot of typing to do, or you like to plug
your machine into a secondary display, a keyboard
may be a good upgrade. Apple offers both wired and
wireless keyboards (both displayed above), though if
you want a bigger, less cramped alternative, there are
some fairly amusing third party options out there, as
well.

Lightning Display

$999 -
**http://store.apple.com/us/product/MC007LL/A/ap
ple-led-cinema-display-%2827%22-flat-panel%29**

Okay, so probably most of you don't need a $1,000
external display, but I'm including it because...well, it
looks remarkably good. At 27", lightning (ha!) fast,
and Apple's unique brand of sexy, this is the way to
do an external display. Alternately, you can get a
Lightning to VGA or Lightning to HDMI adapter and
a MUCH less expensive standard monitor.

Case

Various Prices -
**http://store.apple.com/us/browse/home/shop_mac/
mac_accessories/notebook_cases**

Get a case! Don't carry your laptop around without a case or I promise, you will find a way to drop it. Whether it's a hard case for the actual machine or a carrying case with padded slots, get something. This is my favorite, but there are dozens of options and no you don't have to buy from Apple on this one.

Cover

Various Prices -
**http://store.apple.com/us/browse/home/shop_mac/
mac_accessories/notebook_cases**

Take your protection one step further and get a cover
for your machine. Soft covers or sleeves are fantastic
if you plan on putting your Air in a purse or handbag,
or you can go for heavy duty protection with a hard
case, as pictured above.

Superdrive

$79 -
**http://store.apple.com/us/product/MD564ZM/A/ap
ple-usb-superdrive**

Macbooks (including Pros) don't come with disc
readers anymore. Most people don't need them, but
most people are not all people, so if you need to read,
burn or rewrite CDs or DVDs, the Superdrive is a
must have.

Airprint Enabled Printer

Various Prices -
**http://store.apple.com/us/browse/home/shop_mac/
mac_accessories/printers**

This shouldn't come as a shock (if it does, maybe
have a seat), but Mac makes their own peripherals.
So, anything with a non-universal driver (i.e. anything
not a hard drive, mouse or keyboard) needs to be
replaced. That means printers and scanners. You can
get creative, and some newer printers work
wirelessly, which means your Mac is okay, but older
ones will need to go.

External Speakers

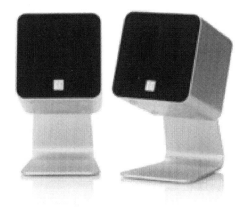

Various Prices -
**http://store.apple.com/us/browse/home/shop_mac/
mac_accessories/audio_speakers**

The speakers on a Macbook Air are actually pretty
nice - not loud but then who would want to blare
music 8 inches from their face. So, if headphones are
not an option or if you're plugging your machine into
an external display, consider these lightweight
external speakers.

Backup Charger

$79 -
**http://store.apple.com/us/product/MD592LL/A/ap
ple-45w-magsafe-2-power-adapter-for-macbook-
air**

The maglink charger that comes with your Macbook
Air is awesome. No bent plugs, no knocking the
laptop off the table when a kid almost certainly trips
on the cord. It just pops out. But, if you forget it at
home, you'd better hope someone has the same
Macbook Air as you because it's the only machine
that uses that kind of charger. Safer bet? Buy a
second one and keep it in your carrying case.

Cable Adapter

$49 - **http://store.apple.com/us/product/MD825ZM/A/lig htning-to-vga-adapter**

The Air has USB ports, but anything else needs an adapter. The lightning port especially is pretty useless these days, so I recommend getting an adapter for any external displays or other devices you want to use.

Airport Express Base Station

$99 -
**http://store.apple.com/us/product/MC414LL/A/air
port-express-base-station**
Any old router or wireless device works just fine with
a Mac, but not always particularly well. So, if you're
unsure about your connection or want to amplify
download speeds, consider an Airport - Mac
optimized wireless routing.

External Storage

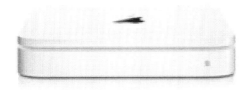

$299 (2TB) -
**http://store.apple.com/us/product/MD032LL/A/ti
me-capsule-2tb**

You have a remarkably small hard drive. At it's
largest, a Macbook Air has 512GB of storage. A
couple years of photos can fill that with ease. Cloud
storage of music and movies certainly helps, but if
you have a LOT of files and want access to them, an
external hard drive like the Time Capsule is a good
idea.

Applecare

$249 -
**http://store.apple.com/us/product/MD014LL/A/ap
plecare-protection-plan-for-macbook-air-13-
macbook-pro**

The ONLY way to protect your Macbook Air is with
Apple Care. Yes, it's an extra couple hundred dollars
at checkout BUT it is well worth it. Break your
machine? Get a new one. Have a problem? Get help
at the Apple store. Don't leave this stuff to chance.
Get an insurance plan that has been proven to protect.

Screen Protector

$35 -
**http://store.apple.com/us/product/H8054ZM/A/mo
shi-13-ivisor-air-matte-screen-protector-for-
macbook-air**

Your new screen is beautiful, isn't it? And it's
guaranteed to get coffee, oatmeal, milk, your child's
snot and a dozen other unsavory fluids splashed its
way. A screen protector will keep it safe, while
ensuring a matte finish that makes it easier to read in
high light.

Conclusion: Wrapping Up

If you don't currently love your Macbook Air, I can't help you.

Seriously, the *one thing* I hear when people complain about Macs is that they're different. Not hard to use but *different*.

You now have the ultimate cheat sheet at your fingertips - a go to document that will guide you from start to finish, from unboxing to on-the-go power computing.

And I'm fairly certain you're going to love it.

Apple might get a lot of press for their iOS devices, but long before the iPhone was a glimmer in Papa Jobs' eye, we had OSX and the Macbook and the machine you're reading this on right now is a testament to more than 25 years of design, development and perfection.

Enjoy!

Printed in Great Britain
by Amazon